For my cousin Lisa Anderson who heard all my exploits and said:
"OMG, you should write a book."
And, when I said I had but hadn't published it, she said:
"Do it."
And for Johnny who still says he wants to be a triathloner like me.

The Year I Didn't Finish

By Melissa Rudolph

I missed it by minutes. Five? Ten? I can't remember a handful of months later. But, my Eagleman debut ended with a SAG wagon ride. I was the last biker on the course.

Two things clued me in early that my progress was insufficient. The first is that a couple in a car drove up beside me and asked, "are you in the race?" I thought they were course marshals of some sort checking up on everybody, but then they turned into a driveway. Random motorists thought I was just out biking as people often do on Sunday morning. They were probably just on their way home from church. I had tried to figure out what time it was by estimating within an hour or so noting the worship times of the churches I passed and whether there were any cars in the parking lot. Maybe their question was really meant to be an encouragement to speed up.

The second thing that gave me a sense that I was not as speedy as I had been riding on my bike trainer for hours at a time was when I passed an elderly gentleman who had gotten off his bike to help a turtle across the highway. Moments later he passed me and cruised on down the road. I think after all that he was one of those Sunday morning bikers and not in the race.

A kind volunteer was trying to pace me as he moved along to remove markers and signs so the course could be shut down. He would ask how I was and tell me what speed I needed to maintain to make the cutoff. But the SAG wagon was circling. I nearly lost control, running off the side of the road when it distracted me by doing a three point turn a few hundred yards ahead. I thought they were coming to get me, but the van drove past and headed back the other direction.

I knew the last aid station was the critical stop. The man collecting signs and cones had told me when I needed to be there, and I had already missed an earlier informal cutoff by two minutes. "Did I make it?" I asked when I saw the truck at the station.

"Well, you have ten miles to go…." He explained the math. I could still ride back to transition, but that didn't leave me enough time to get out onto the run course and make any of the cutoffs. I knew running was my weakest of the three disciplines already. If I had sprinted, I still couldn't make up the time. It was his advice that I stop there to be safer. Kudos for trying to tackle 70.3 miles for my very first live, in-person triathlon.

I turned in my timing chip and went back to transition. The SAG wagon is staffed with the most incredibly kind and gracious individuals. They make you feel like you are a champion for trying, and they implore you to take all the snacks.

My legs are what disappointed me the most. While my neck and shoulders were scorched with sunburn, my legs were ready to run. I knew they could have carried me through the last half marathon of the day. But, I still needed them.

I gathered my bags and bike from transition. Some of the people around me had already finished. Another first timer proudly wore his medal and asked how I was. This was one of the first times I had to tell the story out loud: that I was a DNF after 1.2 miles of swimming and 46 miles of biking. I could hear the announcer calling out the finishers on the red carpet off to the left.

When you Did Not Finish, you aren't ushered into the athletes' post race meal. Maybe I could have used the neon blue bracelet on my wrist to get the boxed lunch my entry fee had already bought. But, I wasn't very hungry then. Instead, I turned on my phone and quickly texted a few family members that I was out of the race, but I was okay.

Pushing my bike and jostling my wetsuit and transition bag was a handful, and I stopped for a moment by a tree. A teammate whom I had never met came up to me and asked if I was okay. I explained that I was pulled from the bike course. Some showing for my team, I thought. They won't want me wearing their name any more.

But, I watched the other racers--the actual finishers--with their family and friends who came along to be what the triathlon world affectionately calls sherpas. I had to walk two blocks back to the grounds of the YMCA where I was camping alone in our family's big

10-person tent. It had been a topic of conversation at breakfast inside the Y. “Are you the one with that great, big tent,” a man asked. “We watched you putting that thing up last night.” Apparently, my greatest success of the weekend would be putting up the tent without any assistance.

I went to shower, stopping first in a stall of the bathroom when my husband John called. That’s when I started to cry. I would cry throughout my shower. But, then it was time to dry off and get dressed in my new race tee-shirt. That’s what I had planned to wear home, but now I felt like a fraud and wanted to take the sharpie I had used to mark my bags and scrawl DNF across it so that no one would mistake me for someone who had accomplished such an awesome feat.

The phone call with John had been less of a pep talk and more a logistical conversation. My early finish to the day meant that I would now be available to drive a few hours away to meet our niece Stephanie who had been watching my mother-in-law for the weekend so that I could do the race. John was coaching our son Asher’s final club season basketball team, and they were headed to the finals of the tournament. My unfortunate turn of events meant that John could now rejoin the team to be there for the last game.

Down came the big tent. In a time crunch, I mostly gathered it and threw it into my van. Away I went to the meeting spot. I tried to think of the successes I wanted to hold onto, the places where I was proud of my effort. I hadn't done much biking on the road, so I was thankful that I had been able to clip into the pedals and take off so easily.

I also realized the things I needed to do better for next time. There was lots to learn and still time to improve before the big race: Ironman Lake Placid. But, there were also still daily challenges ahead.

2

My weekly rhythm is to take Sabbath on Friday. It's supposed to be a day for relaxing and connecting with God. I had also found it to be a great time of the week for some of my long runs. We have a Thursday evening worship service, and I feel like that is the official start to my weekend of Friday and Saturday before preaching again on Sunday.

After the service, winding down for the evening, I got a text from my mother. It indicated that someone had been trying to reach us through her. Ron, my mother-in-law's husband had a terrible fall. He had broken bones in his face and ribs and was going to need major surgery, but at that point no one knew how extensive the damage was. They had sedated him until the swelling could go down and doctors could evaluate the extent of the injuries.

That meant that Joyce, John's mother, was home alone. She had been sliding with dementia that was not yet diagnosed as Alzheimer's. Joyce needed care. "We'll just have to bring her to our house," I offered. It was to be a temporary solution until we could know what was happening with Ron.

That was nearly a month ago. This weekend, because we also had dance recitals, the basketball tournament, and my race, we had enlisted help. Our niece Stephanie had taken Nan-nan for the weekend. But, it was time for her to come back to us.

So, I swam 1.2 miles, biked 46 miles, took down a tent, drove a hundred miles to get Joyce, and drove another fifty back home. I had to remind Joyce that I was her daughter-in-law. She got upset with me for not inviting her to the wedding. "Nanny, John and I got married 21 years ago this week, and you were there." I told her. She laughed and said, "well, I must be demented!"

I told her stories about who had been to visit in recent weeks, and yes, again, John and I have been married for almost 21 years. We have seven children. I go down through the list of who is going to be there at home. I repeated this cycle three times over the course of the drive.

Once we got home, the children raced over to hug me and tell me how much they missed me. But, they had needs for me to fix them dinner and get them drinks.

Triathlons start early in the morning. I had gone inside the Y for breakfast at 4:30 in the morning. By now it was nearly 7 p.m. It would be three more hours before I could actually go to bed. John and Asher returned home from the basketball tournament with the excitement of having ended the season with a win.

I felt a small bit of thankfulness that if I couldn't finish the race, at least I had made that celebration possible by freeing John to go and coach. But, I was on my feet until 10 o'clock. Maybe Sabbath could come Monday.

3

It's a little easier to swallow the disappointment when the marshals have pulled you off the course. At least you know that you gave it everything, and there wasn't any more that you can do. The harder challenge is when a medical volunteer gives you advice not to continue on. This was Lake Placid.

The whole reason I was doing Ironman this year was Lake Placid. But, I will start with a bit more of the full story. Every year there was a big youth rally for church in Ocean City, Maryland. As a pastor in my 20s, I thought it would be fun to take some of the teenagers from my church. We lived in West Virginia, which was only four hours away. I booked the hotel that my parents always took us to--a Holiday Inn. My father traveled often for business, so we used his points to stay there every year for a week in the summer.

I took the teens to the restaurant in the hotel and was astonished to learn that some of them had never eaten in a sit-down restaurant before. They had gone to McDonald's, but had never ordered off of a menu.

They had also never seen the ocean.

It was January, but we had to go down to the beach and put our feet into the Atlantic. At the convention center where the event was, the speaker showed us the most inspirational video about Team Hoyt doing the Ironman in Kona. Rick and Dick Hoyt were a father and son team who were hall-of-famers in the endurance world for all of the events they had completed. Dick would pull his son Rick, who has cerebral palsy. Watching a father and son with so much love and dedication tackle this event truly showed what humans can achieve.

"I can do that." My brain told me that I was capable of doing that. If that father could pull his son in a raft and push his son for all those miles, couldn't I approach the same thing? As a child I had loved to swim and even joined teams year round. But, I had a terrible bout of pneumonia one summer and my lungs were challenged to keep up. I was diagnosed as having asthma, and struggled to regulate it. I was the top swimmer in my age group on my team, but not being able to breathe left me feeling defeated.

Truth be told, I also took up tennis. It was probably tennis that most influenced my decision not to swim competitively. I still struggled to breathe, but being away from the steamy indoor pool and chemicals made me feel like I could get more air. Once I got old enough, however, I took a job at our local park pool. The next summer I took the lifeguard test and was the fastest swimmer in the class. (I'll put my dig in here--I was even faster than World Champion Arm Wrestler Travis Bageant. I heard him say on a television show that he'd beat people at any sport and listed swimming. I chuckled knowing that I had already won that by time.)

"I can do that." It haunted me. I went home and started reading books about triathlons and looking things up online. I made this plan for how I could get to Ironman. First, run a 5k, then do a 10k, then add the Chesapeake Bay 1 mile swim, then the full Chesapeake Bay swim, a marathon, and multiple distances of triathlon until I got to Kona!

I wasn't a runner, though. I knew that would be hard for me. I had gone out on bike rides of up to 18 miles, so it didn't seem too far a stretch to do that part. The swim would be a piece of cake. I signed up for IronGirl, a sprint triathlon and started training. I arranged for a preacher to substitute for me the Sunday of the race.

Then, I had a terrible pain in my abdomen. I went to the ER and an ultrasound showed my gallbladder full of stones. They sent me home with narcotics and told me to follow up with a surgeon. Good thing I had that substitute lined up: I found myself having surgery. This is also the hospital visit where we realized my bracelet had the wrong name and the wrong doctor on it when I was in recovery. Luckily, I saw my surgeon and was alert when he marked me in the hallway outside the operating room, so I'm fairly confident he removed the right body part.

At that point I had felt like I was in the best shape of my life. But, being sliced open takes so much time and energy for recovery. I didn't like the feeling of waking up scratching my arms because I needed another percoset. I decided that pain or no pain, I needed to quit those right away. I felt like I was going to die on the floor of my bathroom. My angel of a grandmother showed up to bring me a vanilla milkshake and the long road of full recovery began.

Life was happening. Two kids, then three, then we moved to a new town. The ladies in my neighborhood did triathlons. They wore shirts from the race I never made it to, and you would think "how fortunate to have moved into a community that could be your tribe and encourage this dream."

Nope. It wasn't really like that. Plus, it was a really hard appointment at my new church. Thirty families had exited prior to my arrival because they didn't want a woman as minister, plus they had a million dollar mortgage on the new sanctuary. I wish I had taken the time to swim, bike, and run back then. I did play some tennis in a league with old ladies who could crush me, and I spent one season coaching the girls team at the high school.

One day, the kids' school sent home a flier for a 5k called the Husky Hustle. I didn't pay much attention to it. But, on the morning of the race, everyone was still asleep. I was up early, so I decided to go down the street to enter the race. There is "couch to 5k", then there is "get up in the morning and randomly decide that you are going to go be in a race that you haven't prepared for at all."

I was so slow. I walked more than ran. I was very last place. And, I still remember them cheering "Go, Mrs. Rudolph!"

I loved it. The running community was full of so many wonderful people. I signed up for little races here and there, and I loved that my oldest daughter Annika ran them, too. She was way faster than me. I would trust that someone would look after her at the finish line until I got there. We did one race where a nun in her 70s cruised along with her probably a full mile ahead of me. Over the next few years, I dabbled in running. I didn't do much actual training. I just liked going to the races and enjoying the atmosphere. I liked running a race in the morning, then wearing my new t-shirt on the sidelines of one of my son Asher's sporting events later that day. I felt less like a spectator than a fellow athlete.

Another couple of moves, a few more kids, some losses in life, and here I was again thinking about running. I had done fewer races. And, I was sick. Really sick. I didn't know what it was; doctors didn't know what it was. They were checking me for the cancer that had taken my father. I was scared.

Because of all of our children, I often had to go to appointments alone. One morning I needed another type of scan. I had to drink the awful prep, and I was certain I would miss the Thanksgiving celebration at my children's preschool. The woman asked me my name and birthday before I had to put on the gown. I just started crying in the little room at Advanced Radiology.

That dear nurse just embraced me while I wept. She told me it would be okay. I prayed she was right. It was over quickly, and I made it just in time to stand in the back of Little Feet Preschool and watch my children and their classmates dressed like pilgrims and turkeys and Native Americans, and tears welled in my eyes.

In the midst of all of the uncertainty with my health, I got it into my mind that I would run the Baltimore Marathon. I had signed up for a marathon a few years before that, but I never showed up to that race. Truth be told, I was probably more prepared for that race than the one I had before me. At least then I had been disciplined to rise in the dark and and cold and run a few miles at the park next door that was uphill both ways. I worked my way up to eight miles of training. But, my son was playing on a football team, and the day of the race ended up being the same day that his little team was going to play during half time at a Towson University game. I didn't want to miss that, and I didn't know if I could travel for the race and be back. It was a good excuse to not go.

Part of me thought it would be cathartic to run Baltimore. I had often gone into the city to visit with my parents when my father would have chemotherapy at Johns Hopkins. Sometimes, I would park at the highest level of the garage and look out over the streets. I joined Team DetermiNation to raise money for the American Cancer Society.

My goal was simply to finish before they shut the course down. My training was more consistent than previous attempts, but that wasn't nearly the load necessary to be a true marathoner. I had never gone more than six miles and I was still developing a sense of pace. But, I left my longest run feeling like I was starting to know myself better as a runner. I noticed that it took me a long time to warm up. The first three miles were the hardest to get through. Then, I hit my stride. I was getting faster every mile. I would later come to know this as a negative split. But, the reality was that I was better as I went.

Our friend Kathryn stopped by the house on her way out of town for the weekend. She had some useful items for me to borrow: a neck gaiter, some gloves for the cold morning, and a pair of goodr sunglasses. These were some good luck pieces. I was also running to honor the memory of Kathryn's husband Jason who we lost to colon cancer that summer, too.

Because I had raised money for Team Determination, I got to go to a gathering the night before the race. Since I called Shaw my coach, she came with me to the event. We were able to tour the house that became a home away from home for cancer patients coming to the

University of Maryland hospital for treatments. I thought about my mother and father driving from West Virginia to Johns Hopkins week after week. It would take them two hours each way. Some nights it might have been nice for them to have a place like that after such an exhausting day. But, I suppose it always feels better to recover at home.

These patients were often there for months of daily treatment. Some were isolated from their friends and families, so the house had common areas that could help people to not feel so alone. Whether I was a strong runner or not, I was thankful that I had lots of financial supporters to raise money for such a beautiful place.

When we got home Friday night, I sat in the bathtub. I looked at my legs and said. “Legs, you are strong. You can do this.” I had birthed seven children naturally, so I knew that I could handle tremendous physical pain. I laid out my clothes with my bib. I didn’t even have good running socks. I scrounged around the mountain of clean laundry and found a matching pair of white athletic socks that belonged to Marley. I had a new pair of shorts and my team tank top.

I had read that I needed to find some clothes that I could discard as I warmed up. I found a few pieces that were in a donation bag that I would be able to wear. I had a running belt with some water bottles, and I grabbed my secret weapon: room temperature freeze pops straight out of the box.

I had decided that freeze pops were a worthwhile fuel since they were basically sugar water. One Saturday morning late in the summer, I had driven Asher to weight lifting for football season. Instead of driving home, I had decided I would run around McSherrystown to get some training miles in. But, I didn't have anything to drink besides my cup of coffee. I had some change and considered going to the Turkey Hill convenience store to buy a bottle of water.

I popped the trunk of the car to see if maybe there were some bottles of water in there. Because we have so many weeks of summer camps at church, there are always miscellaneous items in the trunk. No water, but the jackpot was a package of freeze pops! I took a few with me to drink on the way, and they seemed to do the trick.

They always say to train with the fuel you are going to use, so I had actually completed a couple other runs with a handful of freeze pops. So I grabbed about 10 to put in the kangaroo pocket of my hoodie. Breakfast was a bowl of steel cut oats with a swirl of almond butter and some bananas on top.

John drove me to the meetup place where the Determination team was planning to have a group photograph. It was chilly and dark, and I was the first one there. I waved goodbye to him by the World Trade Center a the Inner Harbor and told him I'd see him at the finish line. There were only a few of us from the team who were doing the full marathon. A huge team of participants were doing the 5k in honor of a friend: they had raised the most money.

I took pictures of each mile. At the Under Armour factory turnaround I could see the SAG wagon following the last runner. I was still in it!

I got to mile 14 and told the photographer I had officially run farther than my husband ever did. I tried to laugh with people along the way for support. One little boy put a ladybug on my arm for good luck. I took a beer from a stranger when I went toward Canton.

One part of the race was particularly cruel. At the top of a hill, someone left a shopping cart. I thought how easy and fun it would be to hop on and ride back down that hill! Another section of the course had abandoned electric scooters. I knew I even had points left on the app that would let me pick one up and ride. I had come this far, though. I had to press on. I was truly enjoying myself. It was an absolutely gorgeous day that was not too hot. I thought about how lucky I was to get to spend the day with only one objective: to finish.

At mile 20 there is a lake. I set out toward the other side, realizing I had less than 10k to go. I could see the SAG Wagon on the other side. I realized I was a full mile ahead of the end of the race. I texted my update to John. He said, “run, run, run!” I was raising my hands and praising the Lord for bringing me here.

And it got hard. Crowd support dwindled, and each intersection I passed I could hear the police radio talking about crossings that were being reopened. The end of the race was catching me. On one street, a man said "man, she is slow as shit…"

I laughed and said, "Give me a break, man, I've gone 24 miles!"

Finally, I made the last turn and could see the finish line. The big clock had already been shut off and the party was over, but there was John and my kids Lydia, Ernie, and Shaw. They came out and ran with me across the finish line. I had so many tears of joy. The man with the computer asked for my bib number and entered me in. He hadn't shut the computer down. I may have missed the cutoff, but I had an official time of 7:26.

There was a box of medals, so I helped myself. Cases of water and fruit and other snacks were there for the taking. There wasn't a lot of fanfare. But, I had my family with me. I had done it. We still had to walk a mile back to the car, and that was the most painful part. I was a marathoner, though. I wear that shirt proudly!

I also thought about the time. And out of the recesses of my memory came the thought that would begin my next adventure. "That time beats the run cutoff for Ironman. Imagine what you could do if you would actually train."

Imagine.

4

"I'm so excited today! I get to go to Cambridge and check in for my big race!" The carpool kids that I drive to school every morning weren't that impressed. My kindergartener Shaw said, "why? You're not racing today."

I had a big smile on my face and glanced back. "Yeah, but there's something exciting about being in Ironman Village."

"How would you know? You've never even finished a race."

Really?

She's five, and she's trolling me. John had told me not to make a big deal about this race because he didn't want people to feel emotionally invested in it. He said it was too much for the people who love me and worry about me to have to steel themselves to follow me on yet another attempt.

He wanted me to defer the race for months. Honestly, it would have been the right move. Even though I put in time in the gym and was stronger overall, it was not a good season for me to race. I had signed up for this the day registrations opened back in the fall of 2020. Ironman races all over the country were selling out because so much of the races that year had been pushed or canceled. I wasn't even sure that Lake Placid would happen as New York was constantly changing their regulations for how to handle the pandemic.

I thought Ironman Maryland would be a good opportunity to piggyback on all that fitness I had gained and would be an option if any of the other races were pushed.

We were approaching two years since I had signed up for Team Challenge. I couldn't wrap my brain around starting another training cycle if I had deferred Maryland to 2022. It just seemed so far off and not racing was a guarantee that I would feel like I hadn't accomplished any of my goals.

My trainer Ricki helped me be confident about all the fitness gains I had made. With the swim I had in Lake Placid, I knew I could do it again in Maryland. I had put in a little time riding my bike trainer. I wasn't training much for the run because of some pain in my left ankle. But, all in all, I felt ready. I even had my tent site at the YMCA booked and paid. The deferral deadline came and went.

The hay was in the barn.

Physically, I just knew I could do it. Mentally, I felt ready, too. It's a strange thing, though, the way that life wears one down in the simplest ways.

I dropped the kids at school. Here is the first logistical hurdle--I had to meet John the next town over to drop my van off at the shop. I managed to do that and get him and our preschooler Johnny back home just in time for me to log into a Zoom meeting that I participated in during the whole drive to Cambridge.

The meeting ended just as I arrived at the visitors center just over the bridge. I could see the flags that welcomed people in all different languages. I found parking and walked over to the village at Long Wharf Park. I went through the line quickly and had everything I needed for the weekend.

Scanning the weather forecast, I knew that this bright, sun-shiny Wednesday was my best chance for the athlete briefing. I sat down and chatted with a man who had checked in a few people ahead of me. He had been doing the race for years--even when it was Chesapeakeman.

Athlete #248 had a bracelet, and a timing chip, and all the stickers I would need for my gear. I went over to the YMCA and picked up everything I would need to come back Friday and set up my tent just two blocks from transition.

I called home to check in. We realized that the timing of my arrival back home also meant that I could keep heading north and attend my daughter Marley's volleyball match at a high school in York, Pennsylvania. The GPS routed me through downtown Baltimore, but I made it to the school as the team was warming up. At the conclusion of the match, I went back to the High School to meet the bus, pick up Marley, and drive back home.

I didn't calculate the miles. But, I left home at 7 a.m., and was just getting back a little after 10 p.m. It was time to go to bed and start the carpool again. The next day was Thursday. It wasn't just another morning to carpool: the main event was the funeral service for Mrs. Audrey who, at 100, had been the oldest member of our parish. It was a beautiful celebration of her life.

I also had to preach the evening service that Thursday. I carb-loaded with lasagna and tried to go to bed early. Friday morning, I drove the kids to school again and told them all I'd see them after Ironman.

Back home, I finished packing all my bags and loaded up the truck. It was time to head back to Cambridge. There would be a window of time when the rain would finish and I could set up my tent. I was glad the forecast had shifted from the expected rain all day because I was already tired from the week, and this was just the beginning.

5

I have the dropoff down to a science. All of my stickers were in the right places--even the volunteer outside was surprised that she didn't have to make me correct it. I wanted to say it was because this was my third race this year, and I hadn't finished any yet. The rain started falling when I got back to the truck. I sat for a while.

Just sitting. I realized I hadn't had the chance to do that for weeks. I don't think that's hyperbole. But, there is always someone at my side or underfoot. If I'm just sitting, it's usually in traffic. This was a satisfying being-ness. Time to myself has been so elusive--not just from the pandemic, but even before.

I often think about when I was a doctoral student. The courses were these week-long intensives in beautiful places like mountain retreat centers. Once, we had an entire day of classes at a gorgeous convent in the countryside of New Jersey. The bathroom had these big, private claw-foot tubs. We watched an Ingmar Bergman film and then had the assignment to enjoy the sacrament of a Holy bubble bath with a plastic cup of wine.

Those weeks immersed in learning and conversation left me so overflowing with gratitude for my life and my family, and they made me spiritually prepared for the months that would come. It was more than being away from familial obligations--it was a time to remember who I was and to simply be.

Soon after that trip I became pregnant with my third child, Marley.

Now, Marley is a freshman in high school.

Seriously? That's how long it had been since I could go away and not be nursing or weaning or watching over others.

A little more rain fell. I finished my early dinner. Soon it cleared off enough to erect my new tent. I had downgraded to a four person that my son Asher picked up for me at Walmart. It was less than ten minutes until I was sitting inside my tent, reading, then napping.

I awoke to a missed call from Kevin. He is my mother-in-law's husband's son.

You could say he's my husband's stepbrother, but that would be a technicality. Kevin has the unfortunate task of being his dad's--and in many ways my mother-in-law Joyce's-- main decision-maker when it comes to care. We had a conversation about the next steps for moving Joyce to a memory-care home.

After chatting with Kevin, I sat in the chair outside my tent. The sky was a shade of coral with a wide strip of rainbow above the swim course for the race. As darkness fell, a little family moved in and started setting up their campsite. Tents and tables and bins. Two little boys kicked a soccer ball around. Then, they started chasing fireflies.

I missed my kids. Johnny loved the lightning bugs this year. He captured one and said her name was Gabby. All summer he would look out over the yard and gasp at the twinkling. “There Gabby.” He pointed. I knelt beside him and hugged him close as he would point. I often talk about wanting to get away and have a break. But, this felt very lonely. I realized that I wouldn’t have anybody cheering me on the next day. The plan all along would be for John to track me and come toward the end of the day. I had optimistically left the bike check out tickets on the refrigerator and in the visor of the van.

Is this where I lost the race?

6

"How are you so calm?" Nervous chatter everywhere at the back-of-the pack swim start. I couldn't give an answer for that. The stranger helped me zip up my wetsuit. A few folks were comparing the quality of ice cream at the Penn State Creamery versus the one at Cornell. Ice Cream seemed like a more pleasant topic than the jellyfish that we were all trying to ward off with slatherings of Vaseline, sea safe spray, and meat tenderizer.

The sea nettles were deemed enough of a threat to raise the temperature for a wetsuit-legal swim. I hate my wetsuit. It makes me lose a feel for the water. But, I made peace with the idea that it was my hope for protection. I really was calm about the swim. Having fought through Eagleman then grown in confidence at Lake Placid, I felt like I could probably have an even better time than I had a few months before. I had continued my weekly workouts in the weight room and knew I was even stronger than I had been then. Surely, that would translate. And, although I despised the full sleeves of my wetsuit, I knew that my split was a bit faster in June when I wore it than when I was sleeveless in July. I just had to keep going.

As I started into the water, I felt much better about how it was going than I had at Eagleman. During that swim I had asked, "what the hell are we doing?" I pictured us all as victims of some shipwreck where we were trying to make it back to shore. I wasn't used to people swimming on top of me and whacking me with limbs. I would flip onto my back and backstroke for a bit to catch my breath and enjoy the blue sky.

But, that would sometimes get me off course, so I'd have to find my way back toward the buoys. This time I hugged the turn and did something I had never done. I held onto the buoy for a rest. I recognized that I had gotten there faster than previous swims. I felt like I was making good time and could spare a few seconds to remain oriented to the course. There were certainly gains to be made by staying in line and not veering too far to the right toward the kayaks.

As I started out again, I could feel burning lashes against my skin. One was on my face above my goggles. Another was the bottom of my foot. Then, there was the sting on my hand. The stings themselves weren't terrible. It was more of an annoyance. But, as I swam toward the next few buoys, I started to feel off: there was some numbness and I was getting nauseated. I thought maybe I was dehydrated. I had fueled up that morning but probably could have used one more bottle of water before the swim start.

I held the buoy longer. I was growing weaker physically. I still had to make another turn or two to even start the second loop. I didn't have the will to do that. I felt like I would vomit, and bobbing around in the brackish water wasn't making me feel more ready to tackle the challenge.

"I don't want to be an Ironman. I just want to be a mom, and that's okay."

I couldn't believe I was thinking that.

I had been training for nearly two years to get to this point, and here I was giving up in the first hour. Before I could stop myself, I was waving to a kayaker. For a moment, I asked if I could possibly ditch my wetsuit. But, I couldn't reach the cord to pull the zipper down. I thought that if I didn't have the strength to maneuver to get out of that suit, how could I possibly keep swimming? He chatted with me about how I was feeling. In describing how sick I felt, I knew the choice I needed to make. It was time to call it a day.

He flagged down the rescue boat and pushed me toward it. I could barely climb up the ladder, which made me see how weak I had really become. They gave me some water and talked to me as they drove to the dock. I watched other swimmers starting their second loops. Some stood in the shallow water and walked for a bit, others kept their position and swam back out toward the marina. I thanked the guys on the boat for their care and presence.

My next stop was the medical tent. I was relieved to see that I was not alone. There were others who were also reacting to the stings from the jellyfish. I recognized a gentleman from the check-in and athlete briefing. He had conquered this race many times, and yet here he was also coming out of the water early. That brought me a great sense of peace about the day. Another woman had stings all over her face and neck. She was angry about the situation because she felt good otherwise, but she had swum right into a pack of the sea nettles. "There's nothing you can do about it," she was finally resigned to the fact that this wouldn't be her day either.

Both cleared by the medics, the two of us set out to gather our belongings as best we could. The racers were already out of the water and getting onto their bikes. We watched as hundreds of our fellow competitors carried on with their planned days and made their way onto the bike course. Some volunteers pointed us toward where we could go. An official Ironman employee traversed some secure areas to grab our run bags. It helped to be able to strip out of the wetsuits and put on sneakers.

My new friend and I connected with her family. One of them said, "let me give you a hug." Her husband let me use his phone to call John. I was thankful that he actually picked up an unrecognized number. I told him not to worry, but that I was finished for the day. I assured him I would check in when I got my morning clothes bag back.

Talking to John is where the disappointment breaks in. I started to cry. My friend grabbed onto me and embraced me for a moment. She squared up with her hands on my shoulders, "listen, you have to come back again. You will do this. Promise me. You will do this."

I nodded. At that moment I wasn't sure that I wanted to try again. But, I appreciated the affirmation and the care.

7

“Everything is hard, but anything is possible.” That is a section of a line in Jeffrey Gettleman’s book *Love, Africa*. He is talking about his time as a foreign correspondent. Specifically, how he can manage to travel the continent and find interviews and connections to the assets he needs to capture the story. I loved this quote when I read the memoir and had adopted it as a sort of mantra.

I had recognized the words on the Ironman website--the company’s motto, “anything is possible.” Surely that was a sign: a part of my favorite quote connecting me to this seemingly impossible pursuit.

I looked at the people who were still racing. They may have been older, or younger.

They may have looked fitter than me or less fit than me. There was no unifying characteristic except that they were still going, and I wasn’t.

I left my friend’s side. She wanted to go and ride her bike on the course anyway. I knew that the best move for me would be to find my morning clothes bag and go home.

The morning clothes bag is just that. It is a white plastic bag where you put everything you take to the race at the start of the day that you will need to have with you at the finish line as well: dry clothes, car keys, wallet, cell phone. All of the morning clothes get loaded onto a big box truck in gigantic bags marked by number. They are all sorted so people can gather them after receiving their medal and finisher swag once they cross the red carpet.

I needed to walk to the finish line area. Moving away from transition, I started to feel a strange numbness around my neck. I felt like my tongue was starting to swell. I knew I was having a delayed reaction to stings. I was thankful that I had not gotten too far. The medical tent was still open by the swim start, so I went back and asked if they had any Benadryl. The medic handed me two pills and gave me more water to wash them down. They checked out my airways and made sure things were still open. I rested for a couple of minutes then went back in search of my white bag at the finish line.

I thought the shuttle bus might go that direction, but it was taking people back to the middle school for them to be able to go back to their cars or cheer on their loved ones who would be passing by on their bikes. I caught up to a family. They were wearing matching tee-shirts to cheer on their daddy/husband/son. The baby had been born in the midst of the training. Everyone was so proud of him.

I told them I was taking the walk of shame because I was already out.

No one lets you call it the walk of shame when you actually put the chip on your ankle and go into the water. This family reminded me of all the hours that I had trained and how so many more people would never even think they could try such a crazy thing. Some days just don't work out.

In my mind I thought back to how this wasn't one day of not working out but a whole season. But the hard reality stretches like this compound. A few more weeks of training weren't going to get me out of this deficit that I was in because of the enormity of my family and life stresses.

The gentleman from the medical tent was walking back in my direction. "Hello friend, it just isn't our day, is it?" I asked. We chatted for a bit. He said, "let me save you a trip--the truck with the bags isn't down there yet." He was trying to get word to his traveling companion about what had happened to him.

For as wonderful a job as Ironman does putting on the events, there is a gap in communication for those of us who are able bodied when we move into the realm of Did Not Finish. We saw staff people gathering up belongings for those who were more serious cases. The ones who crashed or were headed to the hospital for other reasons were cared for. But, for someone like me traveling alone, it is really tricky to navigate all that has to happen to get you all of your belongings.

I told him I was just going to walk down to the wharf and see what I could get into. I knew that at the very least there would be port-a-johns. Cambridge is such a beautiful town. I took in the neighborhood sites and exchanged pleasantries along the way with people who were out walking. It is an interesting phenomenon to be completely disconnected from the technological world and be forced to be completely present in the experience. I couldn't call or text or anything with my phone in that bag. So, I looked around me and talked to people.

One of the aspects of endurance sports that I appreciated from the beginning with the Baltimore marathon is the presence enabled to carry out a singular pursuit. I recalled a day--one I would actually describe as my day off--where I crumbled onto the couch in exhaustion around one in the afternoon. I wondered why I felt so tired, so I listed every single thing I had done that day. As every action went onto the page, the origin of my exhaustion was apparent.

There were 57 things. Diapers changed, meals prepared, loads of laundry. 57. It was no wonder. So, when I was already three hours into the race I realized that it was the only thing I was doing that day. That felt so freeing. It felt like the best possible day. Triathlon carried a similar appeal. I told people that all I had to concentrate on that day was to swim, bike, and run. That felt like bliss.

The downside to triathlon compared to running, though, was clearly all of the accessories. In addition to this morning clothes bag I was pursuing, there was also a blue bike bag, a red run bag, and orange and black bags for special needs on the run and bike. They gave you large backpacks at check-in just to hold all of these transition items.

I did recognize the value of having to prepare all of the items, however. I tended to set out into my days without a lot of forethought and preparation. Getting all of these bags filled and labeled with stickers AND a sharpie in case said stickers fell off was an intense period of focus and preparation. Certainly this also contained lessons for how I could move better through the course of my days at home. Whether I liked the extra accoutrements or not, they were teaching me how to think through what would be needed. I was growing in this area tremendously. I could see where I was becoming more seasoned with each race. I may not have made it very far on the course, but my bags had everything I would need.

When I made it toward Ironman Village at Long Wharf Park, I took a pit stop. Then, I settled myself leaning against a tree. I already had my bike, run, and run special needs bags. So I pulled out a base bar and had a snack. I could see that I really had packed them well. I reapplied sunscreen and even found some lip balm. It was such a beautiful morning to lean against that tree and feel the breeze.

I wasn't wearing my watch because I knew it wouldn't last through the race. It was just me and my few bags sitting for a while. I took time to breathe and prayed for peace to overcome my disappointment. Joggers were running the course. It was still too early for even the fastest racers to be off the bike.

Shortly thereafter, the Budget box truck came down the street and backed in toward the village. I knew that truck had the morning bags. I stood up and walked to the sidewalk. A volunteer sat in her walker smoking a cigarette. I chuckled at the juxtaposition of this bad habit in the midst of this celebration of health and fitness. But, she was one of the kindest, most hospitable people I encountered the whole weekend. She talked with me for a few moments and was such an encouraging spirit. She really was the perfect volunteer.

I stood off to the side as the men unloaded the bags. They tossed those massive carriers. I made a mental note to never leave anything breakable in these bags. As soon as they finished, one looked over at me and asked for my number.

"248."

My bag was near the top of the sack for my segment, so it took no time to have it back. I thanked them for being my heroes of the hour and walked back to my tree. Seated with all my bags, I turned on my phone and started texting my friends who had already sent encouragements. I called John to talk with him about how I was feeling and to get an update from the volleyball tournament.

"I don't want to be an Ironman. I just want to be a mom, and that's okay." That was the thought that kept going through my head on the swim. I looked down at my phone and saw a text from my mom-- she told me my title could be supermom, complete with emojis of all the kids. This felt like a confirmation of what I was feeling in the water as I clung to the buoy.

"Maybe you can get back to knitting." I laughed at mom's suggestion. I'm an even worse knitter than a triathlete. It took me three years to finish a scarf.

Maybe it will take me three years to finish a race.

8

I thought I was at peace with stopping so early. Walking back to transition, a busload of Washington College basketball players overwhelmed me. They were on their way to volunteer. I told them that my son was looking at their school for basketball, so if they happened to see him at the upcoming camp, let him know they met me.

I explained how Ironman works--the distances of 2.4 miles of swimming, 112 miles of biking, before running the 26.2 marathon. I pointed out the swim course buoys and explained that I, obviously, was not winning the race because I had been stung in the face and extremities by jellyfish. They winced and cringed, and gave a visceral representation of what I felt like inside, and it brought me a bit of solace to think that these athletes shared my negative reaction to the experience.

There were more bikes still at transition than I expected. There was comfort in recognizing I wasn't the only one who was a DNF. I noticed something on my bike--bright pink. As I got closer, I realized there was a brand new swim cap on my seat. It wasn't marked with a number, so it didn't belong to anyone else. It was intentionally put there by someone. I don't know who left this gift, but I felt like it was an encouragement to keep swimming and start fresh. I scanned transition and didn't see similar pink or green caps on any of the other bikes. For some reason, mine was singled out. Again, I don't know who did it, but I smiled in a hopeful, not self-deprecating way for the first time since I came out of the water.

I went back to the YMCA and showered in the same stall I had used for Eagleman. That drain has captured gallons of my tears at this point. I hold it together walking through the streets and around the center. But, when that water cascades from the showerhead, I weep. Last time I hadn't packed a clean shirt to wear home. I was certain that I would proudly don my finishers tee. DNFs don't get anything but a few extra snacks from the SAG wagon or Med Tent.

I have a strange relationship with the women's locker room of the YMCA in Cambridge. On one hand it is a familiar place that I am comfortable walking in and out of. But, the emotional ties to the first toilet stall on the right and the second shower stall on the left are an indescribable mix of comfort and sadness. I know I will be okay when I am there: I am able to regroup for what comes next. But, oh, the sadness.... There isn't a better adjective for that emotion. Grief? Regret? All of it and a general heaviness.

I wash my hair. The salt and dirt and general yuck of the brackish river are off me. I think of Martin Luther washing his face in the mornings and saying, "remember your baptism and be thankful." Here in this shower, I hope to be rejuvenated. It isn't really possible to sit long with this sadness because I still have to get into the truck and drive home. If the walk of shame after failing isn't enough, driving home preoccupied with the thoughts of what would've, could've, should've been is even worse.

My grandfather went to the race track every day in his retirement. He always talked about which horse did what and the almosts. I came across a Shel Silverstein poem that I gave to him.

All the woulda, coulda, shouldas
Layin' in the sun
Talking about the things they, woulda,
coulda shoulda done
But the woulda, coulda, shouldas,
They all ran away and hid
From one, little did.

There were going to be thousands of people crossing that red carpet and being called an Ironman. But, I wasn't going to be one of them.

In the truck I took one last look at Ironman Village and the swim course from the bridge. I turned on my favorite podcast *Crushing Iron*. The coaches on the show always give me perspective about training and life. They emphasize being healthy and happy. I didn't feel either of those at the moment. But, I also recognized that I wasn't far off from that. I would live to race another day, if I even wanted to any more.

I was making great time to get back home, and even called to tell the kids I would be there in an hour or so. Asher had taken Ernie to his soccer game, while John was at volleyball with Marley. Asher was in charge at the house. I was outside of Baltimore when I saw the sign for Interstate 70. I started to weep. Weep sounds too elegant: the real expression is “ugly cry.” At that moment, I didn’t want to do anything but hug my mom.

I took the exit and drove to West Virginia. It is about an hour and a half drive. Navigationally, I was simply adding an hour and a half detour. I pulled into the driveway and got out of the truck. I knocked twice then opened the door. My mom was shocked, but I ran up and hugged her-- a nice, long embrace. “Sometimes you just need a hug from your mom,” I told her. She took me into the kitchen and popped a pizza in the oven plus gave me a sandwich and some pickled beets. I told her all about my adventure, and we chatted about everything under the sun.

It was the space I needed to grieve and process my disappointment. It was the space to just be. That was the most healing move I could make because when it was finally time to go back home a couple hours later, I was greeted at the door by children who missed me and needed their own hugs, and “can you get me a drink?” Going straight home to start serving in the kitchen would have been soul crushing. But, having spent time in my childhood home first, I was more prepared to get back to mom duty and get ready to preach the next day.

9

I ran through all of the events of the day that night when John was back home. There were so many people who were texting me encouragements the morning of the race and throughout the day--my trainer Ricki from the gym, my friends Andrew and Renee from Tae Kwon Do. But, perhaps the most uplifting message I got after I dropped out of the race was a dispatch from Malawi.

For the last six months, I had been communicating with Rev. Xaviour Sebastian Chikwatu, a United Methodist pastor in Ntchisi, Malawi. We had started a conversation in a clergy group on facebook about sports. Rev. Chikwatu is a basketball guy, and John and I had met initially on the basketball court when I was a referee and he was coaching (full disclosure, we were not fond of each other at that point for obvious reasons.)

Our parish had recently undertaken a project to help Ntchisi purchase land on which to build a church, parsonage, and basketball court. The purchase had gone through the previous week after some back and forth. The congregation had been working at another site to mold bricks by hand. There were 80,000. Those bricks had been baked and were just waiting for the land to be purchased.

We had authorized some of the funds to transport those bricks from the site 30 kilometers away to bring them to Ntchisi. Rev. Chikwatu was sending me pictures of truckloads of the bricks placing them into a huge pile on site. I could not help but smile. Watching my messenger feed populate with these beautiful photographs made me thankful for what our churches together had already accomplished.

When I was preparing to retire for the evening, another message came through. Ntchisi wanted to name the basketball court after me: The Rev. Dr. Melissa Hamill Rudolph Court. I was overwhelmed by the thought. I didn't think I was deserving of such an honor. There were so many donors who had backed the project, especially a couple of champions who had brought large gifts to encourage others to match them. Surely one of them was more worthy to be remembered for their contribution. John was reassuring. He said, "it should be named for you--you believed in this project." Admittedly, more than one person was sure this was a Nigerian prince type scam, but now the pictures were bringing evidence that this was all real. Rev. Chikwatu submitted receipts for every purchase and documented items photographically. Wheelbarrows and other tools were ready to bring stones from the riverbed for the foundation and sand for the mortar.

As I went to sleep I thought, I might not be an ironman, but I'm helping build a church in Malawi and I have a basketball court with my name. In *The Swiss Family Robinson* book, there was a line the family would use instead of simply saying good night. "Have a delicious repose." The kids and I got a kick out of that when we read the story together, so it has always been a favorite. My tired, pitiful self was ready for repose and it certainly was delicious.

10

Ironman Maryland had been an add-on. I thought that I would ride the wave of all the fitness I would surely gain from training for Ironman Lake Placid. Plus, there was the uncertainty of whether the races would happen in the first place with all of the COVID cancellations. I had rationalized that Lake Placid was my 2020 race, and Maryland would be for 2021.

One thing I had figured out at Eagleman was that I absolutely hated my sleeved wetsuit. My friend Kristin offered for me to borrow her sleeveless x-terra for the next race. I felt prepared for whatever would come my way. The folks I met around my bike at the Eagleman transition were telling me about Lake Placid.

The woman across the rack from me had raced Lake Placid numerous times and was scheduled to go there for a camp in a few weeks, too. “It’s a beautiful swim,” she said. She told me how there was a line running along the bottom of the lake that you could follow to know you were on course. I tried to picture it. She also told me about the pros screaming down the Keene descent at 50 or 60 miles an hour. The day before I had been chatting with an older gentleman who told me about all the times he had raced in Lake Placid and how he would fly down the mountain like a kamikaze. He had also reminded me that swimming, biking, and running are all things that we love to do as kids and that the outcome of the races doesn't matter nearly as much as remembering that it's all fun.

I had signed up for the race in November of 2019. So, when July of 2021 finally arrived, I couldn't believe it was really time to do this. John and the younger kids joined me going up to New York. I had found an inn in Wilmington that had a cottage for our crew. It was a single-wide trailer in the woods that had a welcoming hominess to it that I couldn't pinpoint. It was right on the bike course. Not knowing the area, I was thrilled with the location.

We took the opportunity between bike checkin and race day to do some sightseeing. The ski jump was visible off in the distance, so we had to get up close to see it. We took a gondola ride up to the top of the mountain. The man at the top who helped us unload noticed my Ironman bracelet. He said "Hey….you've done the work. Good luck tomorrow." He gave me a fistbump. It was a nice little affirmation to receive. But, as crazy as doing an Ironman sounds, it's nothing like what those insane ski jumpers do!

An elevator carried us several stories up. We were in a sort of lounge with windows all around. I looked out at the area and thought about what the next day would bring. We still weren't at the top, though.

No, to get to where they actually started to jump, you had to go out on a balcony and take some metal steps up another flight.

I couldn't imagine going out there with just yourself and two skis and holding the position hundreds of meters to take off and fly through the air before actually landing. Who was the first person to even try something like that? Who decided that this would be a standard height from which to attempt something so extreme?

Ironman had a backstory because it had only started in the 1970s. You could point to the original guys in Hawaii who challenged each other to figure out who was the better athlete, the swimmer or the runner--the bike could be a tiebreaker. Over the years in triathlon there were different distances and orders as to which part came first, but there were these guys who were just trying to have fun.

Ski jumping has to have been started on a dare. There had to have been some drunken skiers who watched one guy take off and thought-- "watch me, now! I can land even farther away." Well, this forced me to do some research, and it did start with a Norwegian guy named Ole Rye who wanted to show his men in the army what a great skier he was in 1808. Word got around that people could fly on skis and not die, so they figured out how to do it better and better. It was one of the original six events of the winter olympics.

I wanted some of that bravery for my adventure the next day.

11

The morning of the race it was pouring rain. John drove me into Lake Placid to get on the shuttle bus to go back to transition since no cars were allowed there on race morning. It was out of the way since our accommodations were so close to the Northwoods School where they had set up transition. The lines were long for the buses, and everybody was worrying about being able to make it out to the school and back to the swim start in time. Logistics were changed this iteration of the race because of construction around the olympic oval.

I put my items near my bike and pulled on the wetsuit. It wasn't pretty, and I was thankful that there were not a lot of people around at that point as I shimmied into the suit in the rain.

The shuttles were lining up again to take people to the swim start. I was in the back third of the line. As the shuttles pulled in, someone in an official shirt told our end section of the line to cross the loop and essentially move to the front. We all ran over to where the first bus had pulled in. All of the other people started booing us. "We were just doing what they told us," we all yelled back.

I turned to the people behind me and said, "besides, it's Biblical, right? The last shall be first and the first shall be last."

Just as I finished saying that, the driver informed me that the shuttle was full and shut the door in my face.

"Denied! That's what a preacher gets for quoting Scripture and skipping church on a Sunday!" We had a good laugh at the poetic justice of it all. Some people took off walking toward the swim start. It was a mile down the road. But, some of us just waited for the next shuttle: we would all arrive at the same time anyway. Little did I know I'd end up making the walk back to the beach from transition later that day.

For now, it was thrilling to be on my way to Mirror Lake.

Part of me thought that just getting to the starting line was as much a victory as anything else that could happen that day. So much had happened since that November when I signed up. It was as if a lifetime had gone by, and I couldn't even remember how it felt the first time I went to the pool, or when I bought my bike and tried to clip into the pedals.

I had trained for hundreds of hours. I had thought about this race for thousands of moments. And, here it was. Every month for the last year I had been talking to a spiritual director. Everybody needs one of those--a person who helps you hold space for holy conversations and asks you where you see God at work in your life. He had known for much of that time that I was in training. So, we reflected on the spiritual work that was as much a part of the preparation as the hours logged into training peaks.

I told him that for some crazy reason, I just wanted to hear Mike Reilly shout, "Melissa Rudolph…You Are An Ironman!" I couldn't really visualize that ending, though. I was thinking that to even start the race would feel like the victory. There were so many logistics involved just to get there. Aside from packing my bags, and packing for the children, and remembering all of my gear, I had made the arrangements for coverage at church and had selected the accommodations nearly a year beforehand.

Like anything in my life, there were so many details to sort out before getting into the car. Just that week, we had transitioned John's mom back to her house with her husband Ron, and the next steps for where she would need to go long term were still hanging overhead. I had meetings at church to attend to and even other errands like taking our family dog Andy to the kennel.

But, I was here. The rain was stopping, and Mike Reilly was already pumping up the crowd at 6:30 in the morning. Someone sang the national anthem. I am always in awe of someone who can beautifully execute "The Star Spangled Banner" that early in the morning--each Ironman event had impressed me with that.

The line of swimmers kept moving toward the water. The woman beside me was a grandmother in her late 60s who had completed several full Ironman races. I told her she was who I wanted to be when I grew up. Another woman told me that if I swam in the Choptank, I'd have no problem here.

Mike Reilly was lifting up the human interest stories from the crowd. An 18 year old recent high school grad was enlisting in the military and leaving for Boot Camp the day after the race. A couple who Reilly had married years before were back to race together. Another husband and wife were celebrating their anniversary, albeit apart since he was closer to the front of the pack than she was based on pace.

I got closer to the start, and then suddenly Reilly was beside me with his hand up for a high-five. It felt so strange to be high-fiving anyone in the age of COVID. Then I remembered we had all shown vaccination cards or negative tests, so it seemed pretty safe. Not to mention--this is the legendary voice of Ironman. Yes, I'd take all that good luck that he could possibly offer.

Then I was running into the water. I set out toward the buoys--always yellow on the first part of the loop. I felt the cool water with my arms. I was so thankful to not have sleeves. People were swimming into me and there was the great churn, but people started to separate out. I was passing some folks.I looked over to see some people holding onto the first buoy. Others were resting on a kayak. But I kept going with my front crawl. I swam around people flipping over into backstroke. That had also been my go-to in Cambridge, with a few doses of breaststroke, but here I didn't feel like I needed that.

I thought about all my hours swimming on the team when I was a kid. I smiled to myself thinking about my mom and all the time that she would spend taking me to practice and meets. "I'm still swimming, Mom!"

I went around the red turn buoys and even crossed through a timing arch. Heading back toward shore for the first loop, I glanced at my watch and realized I was making good time. My trainer Ricki had told me my shoulders and core were strong and that I was ready to swim. I was so excited thinking to myself, "Ricki was right! I am strong!" I was still swimming crawl with no breaks.

I was also astonished to look down and realize I was following the line! I had a tendency to get off course, but here I was right on track. The shore line came into view. There was a little section where you had to run onto the beach, grab a drink of water, and hit the timing mat again to start the second loop. And, there I was running. I heard Mike Reilly say "Melissa Rudolph" as I ran on the beach, raising my arms to the sky in victory even here. Had I already met my goal for the day?

I got off course a little as I kept on toward the swim finish. A kayaker was coaxing me back toward the center of the course. I got a little confused and asked if I was still in the right part of the course. He assured me I was on track and to keep going. The kayaks and other boats were starting to circle more and I began to worry about the time. Was I too near the end?

It was time for the final turn. I moved closer and closer to the swim finish. I got out of the water and looked down to realize that I had finished in time! I started to cry, putting my hand over my mouth in disbelief before I pumped my arms in the sky. I made it! I was out of the water!

It was a weird, uphill, run of about a quarter of a mile back to transition. I had to be pointed in the right direction when I almost missed the last part of the blue carpeted pathway. One thing missing from my swim gear back had been ear plugs. There was water or something in my ear that I couldn't get out. I did the hop on one foot and shake your head dance for a moment to no avail. I stripped off the wetsuit, stopped in the toilet, and managed to get onto my bike in a slightly better time than I had at Eagleman.

I was looking forward to a downhill start to the bike, but I wasn't expecting it to be such a technical bit of the course through town with so many bumpy sections. I had put on a long sleeved shirt to knock off the chill because I had never heard of the trick of putting plastic shopping bags in your kit to block the wind initially. Somebody made a comment about how they loved my outfit. I hit a bump and my rear water bottle went flying off. "Shoot!" I said out loud.

A mile or so outside of town a lead motorcycle passed me. The next thing I knew, the first place racer was passing me as he got into his second loop of the course. The motorcycle with the camera was following him. Not too far after that, others in the lead were starting to come past me. Some shouted encouragement to me, which I thought was incredibly sweet of them. "Keep going!" "You can do it!" Here they were obviously lapping me. I wondered if I was in last place. There were bikes still at transition when I left, but maybe some of them never made it onto the bike at all.

Rather than getting frustrated by hearing "on your left" over and over as I was getting passed by the front of the packers, I watched them with awe. It was like being at a fantasy camp where you get to see world class athletes up close--except this wasn't a fantasy. I had lined up with them on the same beach that morning. I had started shortly after the cannon fired, too. I was in this race just like they were. It was crazy to think that I had already swum 2.4 miles and now I was biking.

As much as I was enjoying the beautiful surroundings and the excitement of the race, my ear was still bothering me. There was something in it making a crackling sound and I was beginning to feel dizzy. My inner ear problem was beginning to mess with my sense of balance.

I got off the bike and walked for a little bit, trying to shake it out and restore my sense of equilibrium. A person asked if I was having mechanical problems. I told them that I was just feeling a little off and felt like it was too hard to get going uphill so I would just walk a little bit. I got back on the bike and rode a few more miles. People were cheering, especially at the tops of some of the early hills.

Another biker whizzed past me, and I turned to a spectator and joked, “man, now I have to go catch that guy!” I just couldn’t shake the dizziness. I took another break. A support car stopped and asked me if I wanted to continue. I said I wasn’t sure. He encouraged me to keep going because the first aid station would be in a few miles.

I got to the aid station of the bobsled run. I went past the station, into the training center, up around a loop near the mountain with the tracks, and then the aid tables were set up on the right. I told them I was pulling over. A medic met me and asked how I was doing. I said, “not great--I have something in my ear that I can’t get out.” At that point I wasn’t sure if it was just water or a bug or even some sort of little fish. All I knew is there was something in there that wouldn’t come out and it was making me feel dizzy.

I asked for rubbing alcohol. He said they didn't have any. "Not even one of those little swabs that you clean cuts with?" I asked. I knew that I could at least squeeze a couple of drops from one of those. But, he said they didn't have one. Dean, the man who was in charge of that station joined us. I told him my problem. He also said that they didn't have what I needed. "Believe it or not, I have tampons and pads, but nothing like that."

The medic asked if I had done the Keene descent yet. "No, this is my first loop," I answered.

He got a grave expression on his face. "Then I suggest you stop here." He told me that the pros come down the descent into Keene at 50 or 60 miles an hour. "If you are the least bit off, it's just not safe for you to continue."

I couldn't believe that only 17 miles into the bike I was actually considering calling it a day. At the same time, that seemed like the only logical choice.

They give you multiple chances to change your mind. "Are you sure?" *Are you really turning in your chip? Are you really ready for me to call in your number as a DNF? Are you absolutely certain that the last two years of training are going to end like this? Are you sure you are going to be able to look yourself in the mirror every again and not think you are the biggest loser in the world?*

Perhaps a tad dramatic, there was this peace about ending there. They sat me down in the grass behind the table. I watched as the wave of leading age groupers came screaming in to start loop two. I cheered when I saw a TeamChallenge kit or a BASE kit: gotta support the team, even if you feel like you are letting all of them down.

Dean came over and checked out my bike. He was telling me how nice it was, and that he hadn't seen any like that. I like my bike, too. It was the only one that I could afford because--gee whiz, by golly, triathlon is expensive. It's one of the primary reasons my family has never fully been onboard with the whole notion, right up there alongside the potential for dying. I said, "look how much I paid for your dance/gymnastics/baseball/basketball/school." I'm not a mom who buys fancy clothes or handbags or furniture. I don't even have crafty tools and make beautiful things or go to paint nights or spas or any number of other relaxing hobby adventures.

I swim. I bike. I run. I go to Tae Kwon Do. Occasionally I throw in some tennis.

I was in awe of the athletes I saw coming through the aid station. I picked out the ones who had peed on the bike by watching them douse their laps with water. I smacked my forehead at the very few who were overly-intense and jerky about their handoffs. The volunteers were enthusiastic and kind. They checked on me now and again.

The support crew that would take me back to transition was delayed. The mountains created lots of communication issues, plus roads being closed made it hard to traverse the area. I stretched my legs a bit and even helped to clear some of the bottles alongside the volunteers. But, I knew I still wasn't well.

Thankfully, I had been able to use someone's phone to call John. It sure is a good thing I have his number memorized since I have to use strangers' phones to get in touch with him so regularly. It's so hard to choke out the words: "I'm okay, but I'm out of the race. I'll touch base with you later when I get back to transition."

It was over an hour before the truck could finally get me and my bike. The SAG crew was a father and young adult daughter and another young woman. They offered me all the snacks and were insistent that I have some. They got through some of the back roads and restricted areas. We drove past the leading racers already on the run. Once we pulled over because my bike was almost falling out of the truck bed.

At transition, they checked me out. My blood sugar was fine, oxygen and pulse were fine. They also didn't have any rubbing alcohol, which I was certain would solve all my problems. Someone else let me use a phone, and I connected with John. By then, he and the kids were near the church on Mirror Lake. I knew I could make the walk from transition as so many of the racers had that morning.

I wheeled my bike back to my spot on the rack and switched into my running shoes. Thankfully, all of my gear was right there. I was only missing my morning clothes bag. I would have to go back toward the finish line later in the day to pick that up. I headed toward the shore to make my long walk.

I thought I was sort of incognito, but the kids recognized me right away. They were playing on the playground near the church and came running down to meet me. That's when the tears came. I was so disappointed in myself. All of the other people in town had an excited, expectant buzz about them, but here I was already finished for the day.

The beautiful thing about my family is that it didn't seem to matter at all to them that I had already lost. They were just glad to be back with me. I suppose they were more relieved than anything. They hadn't been convinced that I even could finish the race, so seeing that I hadn't harmed myself irreparably was a bonus.

We got into the van and made our way back to Wilmington where we were staying. I cried along the way as we passed bikers still on the course. *That could have been me. I could have been among them. I should have kept going.* I had really found the perfect accommodations. They could have cheered for me right there on the two loops of the bike. But, I never even made it there once. We picked up a water bottle someone had lost. It could be a souvenir. It was nicer than the one I had dropped in town.

The medics had told me to lie down with my bad ear on the pillow to encourage drainage. They had also given me some medication recommendations. A few years back, John had a bout with vertigo that landed him in the emergency room. Since then, we always traveled with dramamine for any days that the dizziness could arrive again. So, I took one of those and went to sleep for a while.

The kids were anxious to go and do something, so it wasn't the most restful nap. I couldn't blame them for wanting to explore. I got up and went into the family room. "If I can't be an Ironman today, then let's drive to Vermont for ice cream so I can at least check off another state." It was the only state I hadn't been to on the east coast, and there it was only about an hour away.

Not everyone was excited about getting back into the car, but it was a wonderful adventure that took us through some even more beautiful parts of the region. We have always been explorers when it comes to new places. Never ones to ask everybody where to go, we like to read the tourist books and look at maps and see what we can stumble upon. This time our destination was The Bridge restaurant just over the border.

There is always at least one unhappy kid on a road trip, so we did not let that deter us. We made our way to Vermont. The restaurant was a glorious mom and pop kind of place that had the best french onion soup I had ever eaten in my life. We sat outside with our ice cream after the meal. The restaurant was for sale. I hope that whoever buys it keeps that welcoming respite alive.

12

We drove back toward Lake Placid. Now I would be able to search for my morning clothes bag. We retraced part of the bike course that I had ridden. “You rode up this hill?” John asked. “Yep.”

“And this one? Sheesh.”

“This one I walked a little bit because I felt dizzy. Here’s where I stopped a bit to eat my sandwich.”

It was a beautiful stretch of road. Coming through again, I was able to appreciate what I had been able to do. In the weeks following the race, I would see charts of the elevation for the course. The section I had completed was akin to the Three Bears that get all the press later in the race. I had gone up the mountain. It just wasn’t safe for me to go down.

“You were about to get to the easy part--you would have been good for 20 miles.” John said.

That’s what frustrated me: knowing that I had been capable of riding so much uphill. “I rode through here, too.” The next morning on our way out of town, we got another look at it coming from the direction I had traveled. We drove up back into where the bobsled run is. The aid station had all been cleared away. I pointed out where I had spent my morning on the side of the road waiting and watching. Even that couple of miles seemed long in the car.

When we came back from our trip to Vermont, I jumped out of the van at the top of the hill and wandered down toward the finish line. I could hear Mike Reilly announcing the finishers and see the lights. I couldn't bring myself to go all the way down. I quickly scooped up my bag and pulled out my phone to let John know he didn't need to park. I congratulated some of the finishers who were already grabbing their bags, too.

"Congratulations to you, too!"

"Oh, it wasn't my day. I'm a DNF. Dizzy from an inner ear issue. Had to stop before the Keene Descent."

"That's too bad, but probably a good call." One woman reassured me. She told me how windy it had gotten, plus there was a big pileup near the bottom. I had heard of at least one person crashing and needing the ambulance.

I jumped back in the van, and we made our way toward transition. I pointed out where we got out of the water, and the big hill we had to walk up to get back. It seemed like an enormous feat. Even in the disappointment of being a DNF, there is the recognition that I still managed to finish the big swim and go farther than lots of people. There is at least some solace in not being among those who didn't even start for whatever reason.

Transition was open to retrieve my bike and bags. Nobody wanted to come with me. I call my crew the anti-sherpas. They sat in the car while I juggled all the bags and my bike. Other athletes have entourages. My family was just glad to be able to have access to wifi while they waited on me for 10 minutes.

We went back into Lake Placid to buy souvenirs and take one more little trip around town before starting back to Maryland. People in finisher shirts limped around with their families. Everybody still wore their wrist bands to signify that they had been among the competitors. It made me smile to see bands here and there at all of the rest areas, even as far as New Jersey. It was a reminder that we were all traveling together in a sense. If we drove past cars on the highway with bikes still bearing their stickers, I looked up the athlete by number and read off their finisher times.

13

Right now when I open Training Peaks it asks, "what are you training for?" I had won the premium subscription to it from a USA Triathlon virtual summit that I attended during quarantine. I had logged on to watch an interview with Katie Zaferes, the soon to be Olympic medalist in triathlon who is a hometown hero. I marveled at watching her navigate one of the roundabouts in town on her bike one day when I was waiting for a funeral procession to begin. In Hampstead, we don't see Olympians training every day!

My premium plan has expired. Scrolling back through, I see lots of red days for missed workouts. I never had a perfect, all green week. But, I see consistency throughout my training. There were numerous workouts every week. That log holds the first half marathon I ran on the treadmill. It has all of my strength sessions at Coppermine with my trainer Ricki. It has martial arts. I wonder about going in and resetting at the beginning of my training plan with a random date to work toward. I may not have an event to train for specifically, but at least the plan has structure.

In the summer of 2020, I realized why I was really training. We had gotten word that our daughter Annika would have to move all of her things out of the dorm room she and her roommate Ella shared in Manhattan. They abruptly left in March, thinking that there would be a two week spring break to help the country "flatten the curve," then they would be back to school as normal. But, that wasn't to be the case.

In fact, when they left that day, they were never going back into that room. It was extremely emotional to think about what was lost in those months. Because John had broken his elbow and was just finishing months and months of physical therapy, he was in no shape to move.

So, I schedule the move out time and on a particular weekday morning, I hit the road. I drove to Manhattan and parked my big transit van in the loading zone. My task was to pack up and move Annika and Ella's items.

When I got into the room, I looked around at everything. It was just as they had left it. The affirmations written on the mirror were there. Postcards and Playbills decorated the walls. The room was tiny, but they had used every inch of it to contain their lives.

I sat on the bed for a moment and sobbed. This was the time when much of New York City was still locked down. There were few cars moving on the streets. There was also civil unrest in other parts of the city. It felt so dystopian.

The biggest cockroach I had ever seen sat on the sink and stared at me. I took a picture and sent it to Ella's mom. I also told her that we had very good girls because there was no contraband!

Over the course of about five hours, I boxed up everything, threw away all the food and other things that needed to be discarded, and hauled about seven bins down from the eighth floor to the street to pack up the van.

I drove out of the city. I had made a plan to stop for gas in Delaware, but I hadn't factored in the added weight of two college students' possessions in my miles per gallon. By chance, I looked down on the New Jersey turnpike and noticed: 0 miles to empty!

Zero!

I had just passed an exit with a service center. I didn't know where I would be able to get fuel. I took the very next exit and drifted into a parking lot just as my van knocked in emptiness. By God's grace I was in front of the State Police Barracks.

I went in and got their guidance to call for a fuel delivery. A couple of the troopers tried to move my van out of the road, but two college girls' lives packed into the van made it too heavy, and it was not too long before the roadside assistance arrived. I vowed to rejoin AAA when I got home so that it wouldn't cost so much if that happened to me again.

It also turned out that there had been a major accident up ahead. There were delays on the turnpike. What's more, I had avoided being caught in the pileup of over a dozen cars. Sometimes, our delays are a tremendous gift. I made it home late that evening, realizing that I was still a couple hours shy of the Ironman cutoff time.

I also realized that my training is about being ready to go and single handedly move two kids out of a dorm and still drive home. Endurance takes many forms. Some events don't come with medals or finisher shirts, but those are the ones that really matter.

14

Annika's schooling would hardly be the greatest loss of COVID. A few months later, my family gathered to celebrate my mother's birthday. I didn't go to the party at a restaurant because my brood would put the party over the limit. Instead, I went to watch Asher's high school football game.

Midway through the next week, there was word that most of the people at the party were sick with COVID, including my mother, grandmother, aunt and uncle. Everyone was quarantining and fighting the fever and sickness. Granny sounded the worst, and everybody was worried. She needed to go to the emergency room.

I called and told her she needed to go get treatment. "I'll be fine, doll baby. Really I will. I made myself some soup. It will help me." Granny was incredibly stubborn.

She also believed that if it was her time, she had had a good life and would meet her Lord.

It got worse. I called later in the week and told her that I loved her and wanted her to get better, but if she didn't call the ambulance, we would do it for her.

She went to the hospital. I got a call later that night that she was being airlifted to a hospital I had never heard of in Virginia.

The next morning, my brother James called me. “I’m so sorry, Sis. Granny isn’t going to make it.” I talked to my mom and someone needed to go to the hospital for when Granny was removed from life support. I got into the driver’s seat of my van and took off to the guidance of the GPS. Within a few hours, I was signing the papers for the hospital to release my precious grandmother to the funeral home.

The next morning I had pool time scheduled. I had to book the lane three days in advance. I went because you can cry underwater even more easily than you can cry on land.

Endurance.

The daily rhythm of training was a balm for my grief-stricken soul. There were entire days that I felt like I couldn’t get out of bed. I can go to a very dark place when I think about the people who have loved me the most in my life like my Granny being gone. But, I made myself keep those swim appointments. I got on my trainer and logged miles of biking. John even recognized my commitment to train and got me a treadmill.

If you look back through those months of Training Peaks, I have a pretty good routine from September all the way to May.

He had landed on his face and no one knew the extent of the damage at that point. Furthermore, Joyce has dementia (moving toward a diagnosis of Alzheimer's) and she could not be left alone. They had a nurse caring for them part time, but that would not be enough.

We touched base with the nurse and decided that Joyce would be okay alone until the morning, but that I was going to go pick her up in Stafford, Virginia and bring her back to our house just until other arrangements could be made.

I felt like I was going on an extraction mission. I was like the SEAL team of the family, swooping in on these crazy missions.

Endurance.

Joyce needed round the clock care. Our household pitched in with occasional respite from dear members of the congregation like Mrs. Lynne who would pick Joyce up and take her out for lunch or coffee and a ride around town so that she could enjoy the day and so we could just sit for a bit.

In her professional life, Joyce had been an early childhood educator. She never missed an opportunity to tell you that she was an expert. Our youngest children were troublemakers whose parents needed to be called into the office. She wandered the downstairs of our house cleaning and rearranging throughout the night. Joyce would work herself to exhaustion and then have entire days where her body wouldn't let her move from the couch.

She had been with us for nearly a month when it was time for Eagleman. When I picked her up after spending the race weekend with her granddaughter, I had to catch her up on all the news of the family--this included the fact that John and I had gotten married nearly 21 years ago and that she was indeed at the wedding.

It went downhill from there with visits in and out of the hospital for the next few weeks. Ron was making slow progress, but there was no one else in the family who was able or willing to take a few days here and there even for respite. When Ron had been home for a few weeks, he reluctantly agreed to have Joyce come back home. He dearly missed her companionship, but he also recognized that her care was going to require more than even he was ready for after sustaining broken ribs and having reconstructive surgery from his fall.

I drove her back to Stafford the week we were leaving for Lake Placid. She was stalling and didn't want to leave. She tried to sabotage our departure a few different ways, but I told her she needed to go back home now because it was time for my big race.

I knew I had missed some key workouts in the last two months, but also recognized that the stress of caregiving was also a load on my body. I thought that the entire days on my feet waiting on Joyce and cleaning up before she would get to it were enough to keep me strong enough. But, in the end, none of that mattered anyway.

15

When we got home from Lake Placid, the real cleanup had to start. We were trying to find where things belonged in our house after Joyce's departure. When our oldest daughter Annika was a baby, Joyce came to care for her every Wednesday morning. There was a continuous game called "where did Nan-nan hide it?" Anything thought to be unsafe per the early childhood expert would be hidden. We had a clock on the wall of the nursery, but it was hanging over the crib. Joyce thought that there was a risk that the clock would fall down and hit the baby.

I had already thought of that and pulled the sleigh crib out from the wall enough so that if that were to happen, the clock would simply slide down behind it. But, I found the clock hidden away in a closet. I caught her about to attack the ribbons of Annika's baby doll's jumper with a pair of scissors. "If you cut those, you will have to replace the doll!" I argued. There was no reason for such destruction--the baby would be fine. These were examples of Joyce when she had complete possession of all her faculties. Joyce with memory issues was a different beast.

One day, she locked herself in the bathroom to give herself a haircut. I was terrified of how she would look when the door opened. I was pleasantly surprised that when the door opened, her new cut looked fresh and even. I told her it was actually very flattering! But, where was the hair? Not on the floor, not on the sink, not in the commode.... I asked what she had done with it and she just shrugged with an impish grin.

Inside the medicine cabinet. She had thrown the hair in the medicine cabinet when she put the scissors away. Who knew what other treasures I would found her to have placed around the house in odd places. There were some things that I had hidden away to keep safe from the overnight cleanings that happened when I couldn't convince Joyce to go back to bed in the wee hours. Other discoveries were waiting, and who knew when we would ever clear them all.

I felt like I was two months behind in everything, and I realized it would take me just as long to get back to a sense of normalcy in the household.

I brought in all of my gear bags and started to empty them of the contents. Everything was there: my bars and gels and rocket fuel, my race belt with number and tribute names still affixed. I cried over how meticulously it was all organized. I had everything I needed. That is everything but a cheap pair of earplugs that would have helped me to actually finish.

I cried over the enormity of it all--what I had lost, what I had gained. There was still such a weight that I felt I was carrying from decisions about Joyce's care and how to get ready for the upcoming school year that would begin in a few weeks. I cried recognizing that the popular word of the day, "languishing," could not be a better descriptor for what I felt even then, yet I still had another race to prepare for in September.

John was pushing me to defer. In retrospect, I probably should have listened. But, I thought about the Langston Hughes poem "Harlem:"

What happens to a dream deferred?
Does it dry up
like a raisin in the sun?
Or fester like a sore--
And then run?
Does it stink like rotten meat?
Or crust and sugar over--
Like a syrupy sweet?
Maybe it just sags
Like a heavy load.
Or does it explode?[1]

Not finishing haunts me. I was preparing for a meeting and the minutes for the month prior had been the day I checked into Ironman

---

[1] Langston Hughes. "Harlem." From *Collected Works of Langston Hughes.* Published 2002. https://www.poetryfoundation.org/poems/46548/harlem. Accessed October, 22, 2021.

Maryland. The devotional had been about endurance and there, recorded for posterity, were my committee-mates' prayers and best wishes for me to have a good race.

Having tried three times and come up short, I have this feeling I can only liken to when I was All But Dissertation in my doctoral program a decade ago. The academic version of DNF is ABD. I had never planned to be ABD. But, I had moved from West Virginia to Maryland in a new appointment and still had three small children, and my early draft wasn't enough for my advisor to let me continue on toward graduation on time. So, I was in the land of ABD.

In the fall on the sidelines of my son's football practice, I scrolled through my messages to find an inviting one from my new advisor Bill. Suddenly, the hope welled up inside of me. I would press on, even finishing my dissertation on bedrest with my daughter Lydia. I defended it while she was a brand new infant and was finally ready to graduate. No longer an ABD, I was a Doctor of Ministry.

Considering those meeting minutes, it wasn't a good race. And, I know that Ironman Maryland is at a strange time of year for our family life now. But, what do I do now? Where do I go? I go to the Ironman website weekly and scroll through all the events. I don't know why I do that because the dates are already imprinted in my brain. April? Texas. May? St. George and Tulsa. June? Wisconsin. In July, Lake Placid will happen, and there's the spectre of whether it will be the last for that town or not. Maybe this is the last chance for redemption.

Except it isn't. Those mountains will always be there. They were there before humans even wandered over them. The roads were added in the name of progress later, but the lake and the pathways will continue. I can ride the Keene descent any day that I so choose. Hundreds of people do this all the time. The course is already mapped, and there is no reason why I have to do it at the same time as two thousand other people.

When I sit back, the reality is that the opportunity to push myself and be challenged that way is always there. So, what part of the experience haunts me? Is it being deemed an Ironman? It can't just be about a medal and a finisher tee shirt and pictures on the red carpet. If it's really about doing something I know I can do, then why not just spend 17 hours one day and try to piece it all together for my own edification.

That's the question I have to settle: what is the part that is most important? Today, all I know is that I'm in love with the journey, and I have time to go take a run right now.

Afterword

So, why Ironman? I find my answer in Scripture. “Therefore prepare your minds for action; discipline yourselves; set all your hope on the grace that Jesus Christ will bring you when he is revealed (1 Peter 1:13)”. Going the full distance requires discipline, not just for a day, but for the months leading up to it. It requires adherence to a schedule to train the body. It is necessary to put together a plan complete with every detail.

I tend to be a “let’s wing it and see,” “fly by the seat of my pants,” impromptu sort of person, but there is no room for that in the long course. You have to anticipate what you will need at transitions and in special needs bags, you have to have a plan for what and when you will eat and drink, as well as for how you will respond to the unforeseen. You have to carry with you the tools for a tire change and be focused at every mile.

It is the discipline that I need to be who God calls me to be. Triathlon is just the tool to train my body, mind, and spirit for Life. It may not be the mechanism for everyone, but everyone has habits and practices that will help them to be all that they are created to be.

Another hill? I was climbing and climbing on my bike and it was starting to rain. "I didn't know I signed up for Lake Placid this time", I yelled to the racer ahead of me.

"Or Savageman!" He hollered back. It was a nice change of pace to ride with some others for a little bit. It was the next summer, and I found something a little closer to home– a Kinetic Multisports race in Perryville, MD. It was called "Diamond in the Rough." It seems like such an appropriate name. I was doing the Olympic distance race. That is a 1500 meter swim, 40 kilometer bike, and 10 k run.

I felt so great about the swim in the Chesapeake Bay, and I was nearly through the bike when the sky opened up. It was a hilly, technical course. I didn't really have experience riding in those conditions, but I was making my way back toward the transition. It was a beautiful scenic course, eventually winding back toward Port Deposit along the Susquehanna River. A little outside of town, the referee on motorcycle came up behind me. I was the last biker. It felt familiar.

But, they didn't stop me. I kept going, back to the park where the morning started. Here I was finally at transition 2. Were they really letting me run? I threw on my sneakers and headed toward the run course. Shortly after starting the two loop out and back, I passed by my friend Rachel. She was a seasoned racer and was way ahead of me. She had prayed with me before the start of the race, and I was excited to see her making her way toward the transition. "Somebody has to be last!" I was giddy. All I could think in my mind was "I'm doing it! I'm on the run."

The rain kept coming, and the course was a bit messy. I joked with one of the aid stations about needing to backstroke through the puddle to get to them. But, as we wound through the lovely grounds of the veterans hospital along the water, there was so much peace. Before long, I was finishing the first loop and heading back out. There were fewer and fewer people along the course, but one man stayed in place giving high fives.

I passed one of the last aid stations on my way. I thanked them for still being out there for me, and said that if they needed to pack up, they could leave me a water on the little stone wall. "You just run your race, we'll be here!" the volunteer offered encouragement alongside the cup of gatorade.

It was time to turn around and staff members were starting to collect the signs and cones. As I neared the final aid station, there was an unexpected sight. My husband John was standing there holding an umbrella in one hand and a cup of water for me in the other. I started crying when I saw him, "Can you believe it, I'm on the run!" I had left the house alone at 5 a.m., so I hadn't see any of my family that morning and wasn't expecting to see him there.

"Keep running, and I'll meet you at the finish."

"Last runner!" Someone was yelling at the finish. The remaining staff members came to the finish line and hollered and clapped for me. They snapped pictures beside John, put a medal around my neck and grabbed my timing chip from my ankle.

I had finished.

I was finally a triathlete.

They let me take home three whole pizzas and all the snacks I wanted. It was overwhelming to cross the finish line. I missed a cutoff somewhere. But, I completed the race anyway. Journeys aren't always about how long it takes, but being present and taking in every step.

I didn't have any blisters. My achiness was short-lived. My body has felt stronger every day in the few weeks since the race, and now I look forward to what's next. Friends and family shake their heads and can't believe I did all that swimming, biking, and running. They ask me what I'm going to do next.

Faster times, longer courses: neither of those really matter to me as much as the discipline of working hard every day to be strong and healthy. This will now be the year I finished. So, what about your unfinished business? You know what you need to do, so go and do it.

About the Author

Rev. Dr. Melissa Rudolph is a multisport enthusiast, United Methodist Pastor, wife, and mother of seven. She lives in Maryland where she serves several churches and teaches writing and communications. She is also a blackbelt in Taekwondo, which took her 27 years to accomplish.

www.ingramcontent.com/pod-product-compliance
Lightning Source LLC
LaVergne TN
LVHW052051160826
845678LV00015B/3175

* 9 7 9 8 3 7 1 6 0 6 4 3 3 *